TWINS

GURNEY WILLIAMS III

FRANKLIN WATTS
NEW YORK | LONDON | 1979
A FIRST BOOK

Photographs courtesy of:

United Press International:
pp. 14, 38, 45, 54, 55, 57;
The Bettmann Archive, Inc.: pp. 4, 46.

Cover design by: Ginger Giles

Library of Congress Cataloging in Publication Data

Williams, Gurney, 1941-
Twins.

(A First book)
Bibliography: p.
Includes index.
SUMMARY: Discusses the occurrence of identical
and fraternal twins and the growth and develop-
ment of people who are twins.

1. Twins—Juvenile literature. [1. Twins] I. Title.
HQ784.T9W54   155.4'44   78-9954
ISBN 0-531-02265-X

CONTENTS

ACKNOWLEDGMENTS

The author is indebted to Dr. Armin Thies, clinical child psychologist, and Mrs. Felicia Connors, past president of the New York State Organization of Mothers of Twins Clubs, for valuable suggestions they made after reading the manuscript of this book.

I'm also grateful to Jennilyne and Karla Connors, Cathy and Patty Mack, Cathy and Gina Molino, John and Michael Piccinnini, Carl and Frank Santoro, and triplets Karen, Susanne, and Valerie Wozniak for telling me what it's really like to be a twin or triplet. My thanks also to the National Organization of Mothers of Twins Clubs Inc., Rockville, Md., for providing useful information on twins.

GURNEY WILLIAMS III

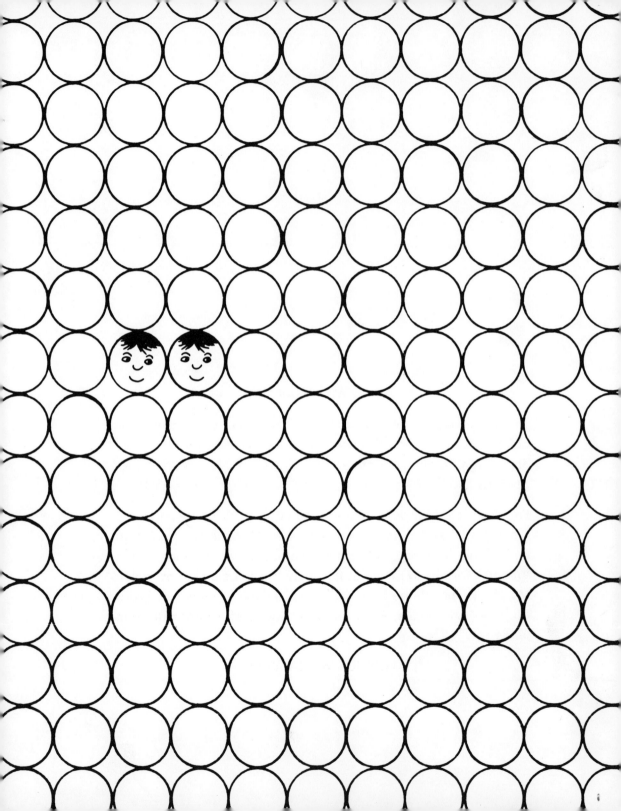

HOW TWINS BEGIN

Here are some of the people you'll meet in this book.

Philippe and Paul Joye were born on the same day in the same hospital and grew up in the same family. But Mrs. Joye was afraid that one of the boys was not her child. Doctors acting like detectives studied the boys' blood and fingerprints, eyes and skulls, eardrums and skin to try to solve some curious puzzles about the mystery twins (chapter 2).

Charles and Joe Crail wrote similar answers on tests in school, and teachers were suspicious. Were the twins cheating? Or were their minds as similar as their faces? Teachers planned a foolproof way to find out (chapter 3).

Twins Carl and Frank Santoro switched places in school one day to try to fool their teacher. It didn't work out the way they expected (chapter 4).

In Siam, twins named Chang and Eng were born attached to each other by a thick, flexible band running between them at the chest. The king thought they were bad luck and ordered them killed (chapter 6).

But before you meet these and other people, let's look back to the time before twins are born. Here's a story that explains what it's like to be born a twin, and how twins happen.

A doctor told Felicia Connors of New York City that he was worried about her. She was due to have a baby in a few days. The doctor thought she appeared unusually large, even for a pregnant woman. He ordered an X-ray to get a picture of what was happening inside her body.

Mrs. Connors lay flat on a table as the X-ray machine nearby clicked on and off. By the time she had gotten dressed, the picture had been developed in a nearby room. There were a lot of people in the room, she recalled recently in an interview.

"My husband, the doctor, nurses, the X-ray technician were all crowded in there, looking at the picture hung on a light board," she said.

"The technician asked, 'How many children do you have at home?' I said, 'Four. Why?' He didn't answer."

Mrs. Connors got her answer when she looked at the picture herself. There on the light board, she saw outlines of two little bodies, one slightly above the other, inside her body. "It took my breath away," she said.

She asked the doctor: "What do I do now?"

"Go home and rest," he said. Four days later, on September 17, 1970, Mrs. Connors gave birth to 8-pound (3.6-kg) Karla Francesca and 9-pound 7-ounce (4.3-kg) Jennilyne Connors. They were healthy girls who looked almost exactly alike: identical twins.

For the Connors family, it was a once-in-a-lifetime experience. Neighbors and family fussed and cooed over the babies. Strangers stopped Mrs. Connors on the street to ask if her two babies were twins. "Yes . . . yes . . . yes . . ." she almost got tired of saying as she pushed a carriage around her neighborhood. At home, the family had to adjust to double diapering and duets of crying around feeding time. As the two girls got older, they got angry sometimes at being called "The Twins," instead of Karla and Jennilyne. Sometimes other children teased them by calling the girls "Twin Towers." Teachers sometimes had trouble telling the girls apart.

Today, in some ways, they are alike. For example, a dentist told them that they had cavities in the same teeth. Their faces look similar. But in lots of ways, they are different. Jennilyne likes mustard on sandwiches, for instance, while Karla likes mayonnaise.

"Sometimes my mother mixes up our lunches and I get the mustard," Karla reports. "Yuck!"

Like many twins I talked with, Karla and Jennilyne want to be known mainly as two normal girls, not as one set of twins. They like having separate friends. They don't like people to think that they are different or odd, mysterious or rare — and they aren't.

After all, there are a lot of twins born every year. In 1976 alone, for instance, 60,664 twins were born in the United States, according to the National Center for Health Statistics in Hyattsville, Maryland. That year, the latest for which the center has informaion, there were about 3.2 million births in the United States. That means that approximately two out of every 100 babies born were twins. At that rate, another set of twins is born somewhere in the

In this family everyone is a twin — no less than five pairs, shown here with their father.

United States every 17 minutes, on average. If your school has more than 100 students, there is probably at least one set of twins among them.

In other words, they're not as rare as people sometimes think.

The way twins begin isn't particularly mysterious, either (although doctors don't have answers to all the important questions about the process). To see how twinning happens, first look at the way a single child — we'll call her Kay — begins.

Kay's mother and father both contribute to the beginning of Kay's life. Her mother's body contains hundreds of thousands of tiny eggs clustered in two small compartments in her abdomen, below her stomach. Some of these eggs are big enough so you could see them without a microscope. But most are so small that it would take four of them clumped together to make a dot as big as the period at the end of this sentence. Once a month, one of the eggs leaves one of the clusters and moves through a tube toward a pear-shaped compartment with thick, muscular walls in the woman's abdomen. This compartment is called the uterus. Most of the time the eggs never reach the uterus. They die and dissolve in the tube.

One month, however, this process is changed. The egg doesn't die. Instead, Kay's body begins growing in the uterus. Why? Perhaps you already know.

Kay's mother contributes the egg; Kay's father contributes a living substance called sperm that changes the egg into the beginnings of a human body. Each sperm is even smaller than an egg. It would take about 600 of them, lined up end to end, to make a line this long: —————— . Each sperm has a rounded head attached to a thin tail that whips back and forth to move the sperm along.

(5)

The father's body produces several hundred million of these sperm every day. They develop in a small sack at the base of the abdomen. During intercourse the father releases some whitish liquid containing sperm from the opening at the end of his penis into the mother's vagina.

Inside the mother's body, the sperm move toward the uterus, at the same time the egg in the tube moves toward the uterus. Most of the sperm never make it to the egg. Millions never even make it to the uterus. But a small number do, and hours after the sperm have entered Kay's mother's body, one — and only one — of the sperm reaches the egg in the tube and joins with it.

Within hours after that, the combination of sperm and egg from which Kay's body will develop begins to divide, again and again, into more cells. This growing group of cells moves toward the uterus. In about three days it reaches the uterus. There it becomes attached to the soft inner wall. It grows rapidly over nine months until it is big enough to survive outside the protection of the mother's body. Then, muscles in the uterus push Kay through her mother's vagina, out into the world. She is born whole, healthy, and bawling.

The process is slightly different for twins.

Sometimes, *two* eggs move at the same time toward the mother's uterus. Then there is a chance that two sperm will join the eggs. The two combinations can then continue on to the uterus, where two bodies develop. The twins that result from two separate eggs may not look at all alike. They may have the same sex, or one may be a boy and the other a girl. In the way they begin, they are no different from any set of brothers or sisters, except that they share the uterus as they develop before birth. Twins from two eggs and two sperm are called *fraternal* twins. Most twins are fraternal.

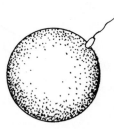

ONE fertilized egg
divides into two cells

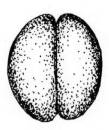

that continue to divide
and form a mass of cells

 that separate

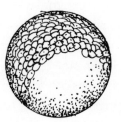

and develop as two
nearly identical individuals
usually sharing the same placenta
and fetal sac

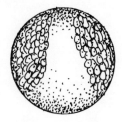

In other cases, a single egg divides in two after it has been united with the single sperm. Each part of the egg develops into a separate person of the same sex. In these cases, the different people from the same egg tend to look similar. They are called *identical* twins, even though — like Karla and Jennilyne — one may like mustard and the other mayonnaise, and even though they don't look exactly alike.

Doctors are not sure why some mothers sometimes release two eggs in a month instead of one. Nor do they know why some eggs divide after joining with a sperm. But they do know a lot more about twins than they knew even a century ago. Since the last century, twins have been compared, contrasted, analyzed with the help of computers, interviewed, and examined sometimes down to their last freckle.

Fascinating stories — fact and fiction — about twins continue to circulate. The next two chapters contain some of the lore and myth as well as some true stories about twins. But medical studies have helped twins and their parents to understand the stories better, to separate fact from fiction.

Today, no twin needs to be trapped in a story. Today twins are freer than ever before to enjoy being similar to someone else, while standing on their own as separate people.

2 WHAT'S THE SAME? WHAT'S DIFFERENT?

A medical mystery story involving twins began in the small Misericordia Hospital of Fribourg, Switzerland. There, Madeleine Joye gave birth to twin boys on July 4, 1941. The trouble began because it was wartime, and doctors and nurses were overworked and tired. Mrs. Joye's nurse hadn't slept for two nights. The day the twins were born, the nurse made a mistake that years later would change their lives.

As they grew, Philippe and Paul Joye didn't act like identical twins. Paul was noisy; Philippe, quiet. A teacher in their school kept mixing up Philippe with another little boy in the class — but it wasn't Paul. It was a boy named Ernst Vatter.

The mystery grew as they got older. Once, someone told Mrs. Joye that Philippe had acted rudely earlier that day. Mrs. Joye said it was impossible: Philippe had stayed home all day with a cold. On another occasion, a month before the boys' sixth birthday, Mrs. Joye saw Philippe and Ernst Vatter together for

the first time. She was so amazed at how similar they appeared that she immediately went looking for Ernst's mother to ask a frightening question: Was the boy's birthday July 4, 1941? Mrs. Vatter said that it was.

Mrs. Joye had seen and heard enough. She went to a local doctor and asked if it were possible that the Vatter boy could have been substituted in the hospital for one of her twins. He told her flatly that it was impossible.

But a short time later, Mrs. Joye had another unsettling experience. A dentist told her that Philippe was missing two teeth. They had simply never come in. A few days later, Philippe's mother visited his school and, while she was there, examined Ernst's teeth. Two were missing.

Now, when the Joyes went back to the local doctor, he no longer said that a mix-up was impossible. A long, complicated search for medical clues began. The basic question was simple: were Philippe and Ernst twins? Had Ernst and Paul been switched by the tired nurse at Misericordia six years before? Doctors, of course, knew what every six-year-old child knew: Philippe and Ernst *looked* alike. But identical twins are similar in many other ways. In months of investigation, doctors began checking off the ways.

One test: researchers took small amounts of blood from Mrs. Vatter and her son (Mr. Vatter had died recently) and all the members of the Joye family. The doctors examined the blood carefully. The initial blood test proved nothing because everyone in the two families had the same blood type.

Another test: when Philippe and Ernst were born, how much did they weigh? Twins tend to be smaller at birth than single babies. If Ernst were a twin, his birthweight might have been comparatively low. Researchers delved into old hospital charts. They found Mrs. Joye's record, and it contained another clue. Paul's weight was given as 3,180 g (7 pounds) — a normal weight for a single child. But next to the handwritten numerals, the investigators could read another weight, which someone had erased. It read "2,470 g." That was about 5½ pounds — not an unlikely weight for a twin. It looked as though someone had switched Paul for Ernst one day, and then rewritten the weights.

Neither the initial blood test nor the weight *proved* that the twins had been switched. Nor did the series of tests that followed, although each test showed more similarities between Philippe and Ernst. Doctors found that their fingerprints were alike. Comparisons of their eyes, skulls, and even their eardrums showed further similarities.

None of these tests, however, was accepted as final proof. People can be alike in many ways and still not be identical twins.

A final test settled the question of the mysterious twins. The bodies of identical twins have a remarkable ability to share skin. Suppose one identical twin — we'll call her Sarah — is so badly burned on the leg that her skin can't grow back and heal the wound. Then her twin sister, Cynthia, can donate some of her own skin to patch the wound. In a fairly simple operation, doctors will put Cynthia to sleep and cut from her leg a layer of skin thin enough so that Cynthia's skin will grow back. Then they will apply the layer to Sarah's wound. Friends and brothers and sisters who aren't identical twins can't make a donation like this to someone else. But identicals are so alike that Cynthia's skin will continue living on Sarah's leg, closing up the burned area.

In the final test on Philippe, Paul, and Ernst, doctors cut small patches of skin from each boy and traded the patches. The layer of skin on Paul's body died and fell away. The transplanted skin on Philippe and Ernst stayed alive.

Now there could be no doubt. Philippe and Ernst were identical twins. Paul belonged legally with the Vatter family. The transfer was made, and after some difficult adjustments, the three boys learned to like their newly arranged families. Writer George Kent, who told this true story in the November, 1951, *Reader's Digest*, reported that one day after the transfer, Ernst looked at Philippe and said, "I have found the other half of me." (You can get more information on where to find this and other stories told in this book by checking the final section, "For Further Information.")

The case of the mixed-up twins illustrates some of the ways identical twins are alike. They look alike. They have the same color eyes and hair and skin. Natural chemicals in their blood are the same. One can donate skin to the other.

Those are all physical similarities. Do twins have similar minds? Do they think and act alike?

Those are much tougher questions to answer. Identical twins themselves often argue that they are completely different from each other, no matter what anyone says. Take John and Michael Piccinnini of New York City, for example. They are identical twins, born December 8, 1966. When they were interviewed at the age of eleven, they said adults — even their own parents — sometimes had trouble telling them apart. Their mother, for example, sometimes plays it safe by using both names when telling one of the twins what to do. She'll say, "Michael, pick up your clothes, John."

The confusion goes back to when the boys were infants. One day when he was a baby, John said, his mother fed him twice

and skipped Michael's feeding because she couldn't keep straight who was who.

The important thing is, *they* don't think they look alike, and young children — like their five-and-a-half-year-old sister Maria — have no trouble telling who is John and who is Michael. Neither does their pet dog, Rusty, a golden retriever.

"I look in the mirror," John said, "and I see myself, and then I look at Michael, and I say, 'How could anyone ever get mixed up?' " There are dozens of differences between them, both of them said. Michael likes chocolate ice cream while John likes strawberry, for instance. John hates pickles. Michael loves them.

·Researchers who have studied twins closely have discovered many similarities besides the way they look. In general, twins tend to have similar scores when they are tested for intelligence. Their scores tend to be more alike than the scores of brothers and sisters who are not twins. And identical twins tend to be more alike in intelligence than fraternal twins. (The previous chapter describes the difference between the two types of twins.) Other studies have shown similarities in twins' temperament.

This and other research show that twins can be alike in many ways. But twins themselves, like John and Michael, will tell you how different they are from each other.

These identical twins lost
front teeth at the same time.
Then one fell, breaking her
left arm. A few days later the
other fell and broke her left arm.

In interviews with several sets of twins, one said: "I'm neat, my sister's messy." Another: "When I feel happy, my brother feels sad." Another: "My brother's good at sports; I'm good at reading." The point is (and little sister Maria and a dog named Rusty already know the point), even though John and Michael are alike in some ways, if you know John, you don't necessarily know Michael.

Another set of questions about similarities and differences: Are twins different from single children? Are they smarter? Bigger? Healthier? Happier?

The simple answer is that twins aren't as different from other children as people sometimes think they are. According to Amram Scheinfeld, a writer and an expert on twins, their scores on intelligence tests are about the same as scores of nontwins. Many twins are born with low birthweights — many weigh less than 5½ pounds (2.5 kg) at birth — and they may be lighter and shorter than other children. But these differences disappear for the most part as they grow up.

Do twins tend to be healthier or suffer more illness? The answer is that twins tend to have more health problems at *birth* because of their smaller size. But once they have made it successfully through birth, most twins don't have any more health problems than anyone else.

Are they happier, or are they "problem children"? Scheinfeld said his surveys of hundreds of twin families showed that twins were at least as happy as single children in the same family.

Again, there's nothing mysterious about twins, even though for centuries many people have believed weird stories and myths about children born together. The next chapter retells some of those stories.

TWIN LORE
AND LEGEND

The story is told of a famous American judge named Charles S. Crail who had an identical twin brother named Joe. In school, teachers suspected the two boys of cheating because their answers on written tests were often alike. The twins had been separated as far as possible in the classroom, but their answers to test questions remained suspiciously similar.

One day, when the boys faced a Latin exam, teachers made them go to different rooms for the test to prevent cheating. Joe Crail went to the principal's office. Charles Crail went to a teacher's office. Charles was given the exam. But he refused to start work. He said that he wasn't ready. He sat stock still for about half an hour, without lifting a pencil, while the teacher got impatient. Finally, the principal appeared in the teacher's office. The principal said he had lost the exam, and that he had been too busy for the past half-hour to get Joe started on the test. With the teacher's help, Joe got his copy of the exam and, finally, both brothers began to write.

(17)

At noon, the story goes, the principal called the boys into his office. He said that he was certain there had been no cheating on other tests. The papers turned in that morning by both boys were identical. They had even made the same mistakes.

That's a story from the twentieth century— it was published in 1932 by Crail himself, who said it was true. It's typical in some ways of stories that have been told about twins for centuries. For thousands of years, some people have held beliefs that twins had strange powers, sometimes for good, sometimes for evil.

Even in this century, for example, some tribes in Upper Guinea in Africa have treated twins like superheroes. Twins had to live in special houses, built by other twins. They wore white beads. Members of the tribe believed that twins could predict the sex of unborn children. They also thought that twins could survive bites by poisonous snakes, and that they could stop water from boiling, simply by flexing their minds.

One tribe in California, called the Cocopa, believed that all twins come from the heavens and only appear on earth as visitors. The tribe believed twins deserved special care because if they didn't get it, they might go back home to the heavens.

Other tribes, however, thought twins were evil spirits. Some put twins to death right after birth, and some killed the mother as well. The murderers believed wild myths that twins had been sent by enemy tribes.

Many of the myths about twins as superheroes — or villains — have died as scientists have discovered how twins really begin. But some weird stories persist about how twins have performed miraculous feats or found each other after long separations.

Writer Bard Lindeman tells the story, for example, of twins named Roger Brooks and Tony Milasi. They were brought up in different homes. Then, as young men, they met each other and made a series of surprising discoveries. It wasn't so much that their voices sounded alike or that they looked alike — many identical twins shared such similarities. But the two men were amazed to find that they both used the same brand of Danish toothpaste and smoked the same kind of cigarettes.

Twin writers Dr. Judy Hagedorn and Dr. Janet Kizziar of Oklahoma tell of another case of identical twins separated at birth. When they finally caught up with each other as adults, they found that both of them were telephone repairmen. That wasn't all. Without knowing anything about the other twin, each had gotten married in the same year. Most surprising, both had adopted fox terriers as pets. And both dogs were named Trixie.

Another story of curious coincidence: a French soldier was badly burned in battle during World War II and rushed to a hospital. The burns were so deep that the skin could not grow back by itself. His life was in danger. So some of the staff of the hospital were amazed a few days later to see the soldier walking around, healthy and cured.

The man they saw was the soldier's identical twin, who just happened to be in the hospital at the same time his brother was admitted. It was a stroke of good luck for the brother. Doctors took patches of skin from the healthy man — who was able to regrow the missing patches — and donated the skin to cover the wounds of his brother. The soldier survived with the help of his twin.

All of these stories seem to be saying the same thing: Twins have some mysterious powers. Primitive tribes thought the powers had something to do with heaven or the world of spirits. Some people today think twins can communicate messages with their minds, sometimes over long distances, sometimes without even knowing it.

But scientists today have taken a hard look at claims of mystical abilities and curious coincidences, and the scientists are skeptical. Dr. Joseph B. Rhine, for one, has tested whether twins have any more ability than anyone else to send and receive thought without speech or visible signal.

In a typical test used by Dr. Rhine, one person stares at a printed card with a bold design, such as a star. A second person sits out of sight of the first and tries to imagine what the first person is seeing. In one test, or "run," of course, many people are able to guess the pattern from sheer luck. But Rhine looks for more than luck. He estimates before each run how many right answers a test subject is likely to give just by lucky guesses. When subjects score far above his predictions, Rhine and others think such tests show that some kind of invisible mental signal is at work.

What has Rhine found about twins? Nothing outstanding. Twins, he has reported, have no greater power of mental communication than any other set of brothers or sisters, or even pairs of friends.

So how can you explain what happened to Judge Crail and his twin, who seemed to be able to send Latin words through space? Why did the twin telephone repairmen choose the same name for their pet terriers? Was it just coincidence that the burned soldier was sent to the same hospital as the twin brother who had the power to save him? No one knows for sure. Maybe, since identical twins are alike in many ways, they often tend to think along the same lines, even though they don't actually send thoughts like radio signals. Sometimes even brothers and sisters who *aren't* twins seem to be able to read each other's thoughts, just because they know each other so well. In other cases, there is probably nothing more than chance at work. None of the twins I talked to thought he or she had mystical abilities. None felt mysterious signals flowing back and forth, although several families reported curious coincidences of their own. (The next chapter contains some of their reports.) Some future scientist may be able to explain such coincidences as easily as doctors today can explain, without magic, many of the details of how twins begin. Some stories about twins, on the other hand, will never be explained scientifically.

They aren't meant to be.

Henry Sambrooke Leigh, a writer in the last century, once wrote a funny story in verse about being an identical twin. It starts in a silly fashion and runs on to a mind-bending ending:

THE TWINS

In form and feature, face and limb, I
   grew so like my brother,
That folks got taking me for him,
And each for one another.
It puzzled all our kith and kin,
It reached a fearful pitch;
For one of us was born a twin,
Yet not a soul knew which.

One day, to make the matter worse,
Before our names were fixed,
As we were being washed by nurse,
We got completely mixed;

And thus, you see, by fate's decree,
Or rather nurse's whim,
My brother John got christened me,
And I got christened him.

This fatal likeness even dogged
My footsteps when at school,
And I was always getting flogged,
For John turned out a fool.
I put this question, fruitlessly,
To every one I knew,
"What *would* you do, if you were me,
To prove that you were *you*?"

Our close resemblance turned the tide
Of my domestic life,
For somehow, my intended bride
Became my brother's wife.
In fact, year after year the same
Absurd mistakes went on,
And when I died, the neighbors came
And buried brother John.

The American humorist Mark Twain composed a similarly silly report, pretending in an interview with a newspaper reporter that he was a twin who had gotten mixed up in the bathtub with his identical brother. As retold by Hal Holbrook in *Mark Twain Tonight!* Twain is responding to a reporter about whether he has any brothers.

"Oh. Yes, now that you mention it; there was a brother William — *Bill* we called him. Poor old Bill!"

"Why? Is he dead?"

"We never could tell. There was a great mystery about that, you see."

"That is sad. He disappeared, then?"

"Well, yes, in a sort of general way. We buried him."

"*Buried* him! Without knowing whether he was dead or not?"

"Oh, no. He was dead enough, all right. You see, we were twins — defunct and I — and we got mixed up in the bathtub when we were only two weeks old, and one of us was drowned. But we didn't know which. Some think it was Bill. Some think it was me."

"What do you think?"

"I would give worlds to know. This solemn, this awful mystery has cast a gloom over my whole life. But I'll tell you a secret which I've never revealed to anyone before. One of us had a peculiar mark — a large mole on the back of his left hand; that was *me*. That child was the one that was drowned."

4 WHAT IT'S REALLY LIKE TO BE A TWIN

Carl and Frank Santoro, identical twins born January 30, 1966, are on a terrific basketball team in Queens, New York. When they were interviewed, they had won thirty-eight games straight.

It's happened more than once on the basketball court: Carl has the ball, and a player on the other team is guarding him, man on man. Suddenly, Frank gets in front of Carl, solid as a post. Carl breaks toward the basket. Frank stands in the way of the player from the other team. Carl is free to shoot. The ball is up. He scores.

It's one of the advantages of being a twin that the two boys can run the play — it's called "setting a pick" — without much planning. They know what to do, partly because they're twins and they've been on the same family "team" all their lives.

But sometimes being a twin on the same team doesn't work out. In one tournament game, Frank scored the first two points of the first period. But the scorer mixed up the twins and gave Carl the credit for the points. The final score was close — 43-39 — so Frank's points made a big difference.

"It didn't bother me that much," Frank said later, "because I knew I had made those points." But it would have been nice if the adult could have gotten things straight and given him the points he had made.

All the twins I talked with had the same kind of story. All of them liked being twins, sometimes. All disliked it, sometimes. All of them had a few complaints about the way people talked to them. A couple had surprising stories about how they seemed to know what the other was thinking.

What's it really like being a twin? Here's what twins themselves — around the age of eleven or twelve — reported.

WHAT'S GOOD ABOUT BEING A TWIN?

Frank Santoro: "Today in class, Carl forgot his assignment pad. So I lent him mine." Being a twin often means you have someone nearby to help you when you need it.

Carl Santoro: "When Frank is playing baseball and he's up at bat, I really want him to get a hit, and I'm really glad when he does." Being a twin often means you have someone to cheer for you.

Mrs. Santoro: "I have twin brothers myself, and they've always been very close. They used to have a good time in school. Their handwriting was so similar that one time one of the twins took a test in place of the other. He passed the test for his brother.

"Another time in a basketball game, one of the brothers made five fouls and the ref told him to leave the game. 'It's not me!' he said. 'It's my brother!' The crowd loved it." Being a twin means people are interested in you, and they're inclined to want to know more about you.

Does being a twin mean you can play tricks and fool people about who you are? Some twins I talked with said they had switched places sometimes for fun — but it wasn't as much fun as they thought it would be.

One day years ago, for instance, Frank and Carl plotted out how they would change classrooms in school. Before the switch, they talked over where they sat and what they did, and when they got to school, each twin went to the other twin's classroom.

It was fun for about two seconds. Then Carl got nervous. "I'm Frank," he told himself. Then he started to say it aloud. "I'm Frank! I'm Frank!" He was trying to remember the part he was supposed to play. It didn't take long for everyone to discover that the boy saying "I'm Frank!" wasn't Frank. The twins switched back after about five minutes.

More often, twins play games like regular friends. Karla and Jennilynne Connors, for example, are pretty evenly matched on board games like Concentration, and they both like having someone to play with whenever they want. But they don't have to play together; each has a different set of friends.

So do twins Michael and John Piccinnini. And another advantage of being twins, from their point of view, is that you get to know a lot of people like you. "I meet all of John's friends," Michael said. "And if I invite someone over, I introduce him to John. So you wind up meeting a lot of people your age. You inherit friends you wouldn't have if you weren't a twin."

Being a twin, in other words, is fun sometimes.

And sometimes it isn't.

WHAT'S HARD ABOUT BEING A TWIN?

Carl Santoro: "One time I was watching TV and my father was asleep. Frank snuck up behind me and put his hand over my mouth and made a lot of noise and my father woke up. He got mad at me because for a second he couldn't tell us apart."

That was a common complaint. Identical twins often get tired of being confused with someone else.

John Piccinnini: "Michael and I were in the same reading class once, and this teacher looks at Michael to have him read out loud. She's looking right at him and she calls 'John.' So I start reading, all the way across the room. The teacher didn't apologize or anything."

Some people think it's funny to mix up twins on purpose. When John and Michael were about four years old, for instance, one woman switched their names whenever she saw them. "Hello, Michael," she would say to John. No one in the twins' family thought it was funny. After a few minutes with this woman, the four-year-old boys themselves got confused and scared about who they were. Their mother had to tell the woman to stop teasing her sons.

There are times when twins resent looking like someone else. One set of identical twins I talked with tried to solve the problem by wearing different colors. One wore reds and browns. The other wore blues and greens. They reported that the color signals did help people to keep them straight, but one of the twins said he didn't like the system much. "I hate it when people have to go by the clothes we wear to tell who we are," he said.

Twins agreed that it wasn't hard to make friends. But being a twin sometimes means you aren't treated as a regular friend. Several sets reported, for instance, that their friends were hesitant to invite one twin to a party or to spend the night because they thought they would have to invite the other twin at the same time. Some twins wanted to send a message to the world: "If you invite one, you *don't* have to invite the other." Other twins are used to being invited everywhere together. The point is that just because someone is a twin doesn't necessarily mean you have to invite a brother or sister, too, if there's only room for one.

WHAT TWINS DON'T LIKE TO HEAR

One hard part about being a twin is listening to the same old questions and jokes.

It happens all the time: identical twins are walking down the street, dressed in identical sneakers, faded jeans, and blue shirts. Their hair hangs over their ears. Their eyes are the same color. They both wear glasses. They are about the same height and weight. Their faces look alike. And a stranger stops them to ask: "Hey, are you twins?"

Some twins get a little tired of being asked. One Mothers of Twins Club in Des Moines, Iowa, drew up some answers to the question a few years ago that twins themselves can adapt when they are asked if they are twins.

One answer: "No, we're a pair of identical strangers."

A second response: "Nope, I'm an only child. Who's your eye doctor?"

Patty Mack of New York City has another complaint about what she doesn't like to hear. She's the twin sister of Cathy Mack. Both were born on January 31, 1967. "People are always asking, 'Who's the oldest?' And Cathy always says, 'I am.'" Cathy is right, but Patty thinks everybody ought to know just how much older Cathy is: "About a minute," Patty explains.

Gina and Cathy Molino, identical twins born December 15, 1966, said kids in their school often make a big fuss over them — more of a fuss than they really enjoy. "Sometimes in school kids scream, 'Let me guess! Let me guess!' acting as though they can't tell us apart," Gina said, even though Gina wears her hair long and Cathy wears it short. Cathy added: "Sometimes people we haven't met will say, 'Are you twins?' And when we say yes, they ask when I was born, and I tell them, and then they ask when Gina was born." She thinks people ought to know that twins usually have the same birthday.

Gina agreed. "Sometimes I want to scream," she said.

John and Michael Piccinnini feel the same way about people who talk to them and treat them as if they were one person. If someone's passing out candy, for instance, they give one piece to John and say, "You're a twin. You can share."

Several of the twins said they didn't even like being called "The Twins." Their real names, they said, would do just fine.

"I'm not special," one said. "And I'm not the same as my brother."

THE CURIOUS SIDE OF BEING A TWIN

Still, some of the twins I talked with had some unusual stories to tell. Even though most liked to be known as different people, some reported rare experiences in which they seemed to think and feel like one person.

When John and Michael Piccinnini were about eighteen months old, for instance, John fell downstairs one day and cut his head. Without telling Michael about the fall, someone took Michael to a neighbor's house to stay while John was rushed to a doctor. Michael had visited the neighbor's house by himself many times. He was usually happy to go. But the day John fell, Michael was restless. He kept asking for his brother, and fretted and cried until John came home, with three stitches in his head.

His family said Michael acted as though he knew John was in trouble.

Felicia Connors reports the same kind of thing happened when her identical twins were about eighteen months old. Jennilyne woke up screaming one night, rousing the whole family. Karla was quiet in her crib. No one could find anything wrong with Jennilyne, but Karla was hot and feverish in the other crib. A doctor hospitalized her the next morning. X-rays showed that she had a broken collarbone, and the family later figured out she must have fallen while playing the previous day. But Jennilyne was the one who cried.

Marcia Santoro reported several other examples of twins in tune with each other. When her twin brothers visited the World's Fair in New York in the mid-1960s, they went with her to the fairgrounds on different days. She noticed that something unusual was happening a few minutes after starting her second visit.

"My brother would point at something at the fair, or say something about how it looked to him, and I'd tell him I had heard that comment before. I kept saying, 'Your brother said the same thing a week ago.' It was eerie how much they thought alike."

As her brothers were growing up, she added, the same kind of thing often happened when they went shopping for clothes. One would buy a suit, without his brother's knowledge. A week later, the twins would dress for a party. And when they were ready — you can probably guess — both would be wearing the same suit.

This kind of thing doesn't happen to all twins. Many have never had unusual experiences. On the other hand, brothers and sisters who aren't twins have sometimes gone through periods where they thought or acted like a close relative in the same family.

Once again, there probably isn't as much mystery here as some people think. Twins are alike in lots of ways. So it's not too surprising that twins sometimes act alike, or think on the same wavelength, even though they remain separate people.

The first two chapters report some of the ways twins are alike, and different. Scientists pay a lot of attention to these similarities and differences because — as the next chapter reports — studies of twins tell us a lot about all people, twins and nontwins.

HOW TWINS HELP YOU

What makes you the person you are? Why do some people tend to be on the go all the time, while others tend to sit on the sidelines? Why do some people work at puzzles until they finish them, while others yell, "Stupid!" at puzzles and throw them away? Why do some kids like to eat just about anything put on their plates, while others are picky?

Twins can help answer these questions. Scientific studies of twins can help all of us, twins and nontwins, understand how we got to be the people we are. How? And what are the answers to the questions?

To begin with, many things make you the person you are. Maybe you feel crabby today, for instance, because somebody yelled at you in school. Or maybe you feel itchy and want to move in your seat, just because you *always* feel like moving. Maybe you're a good baseball player because your mother or father started playing catch with you when you were young. Or maybe you got a hit the first time you went to bat without ever playing ball before, as spectators in the stands told each other you were a "born athlete."

Many scientists today think all of the things that make you who you are really come down to two important things.

One: you *inherit* a lot from your family. If your mother and father have blue eyes, for instance, you have blue eyes, by inheritance. There's more to it than that. In addition to looking like a parent or other family member, you may be like a close relative in other ways. It's possible, for instance, to inherit intelligence.

The second thing: you're shaped by the world of people, places, things, and actions around you, by your *environment*. You learned to speak English, for instance, in part because people spoke it around you. You learned not to blow bubbles in the bottom of an ice-cream soda glass because your family blew up at you if you did. The way you dress, the length of your hair, the way you pronounce certain words — all of these parts of you depend on your environment.

Which do you think is more important, *inheritance* or *environment,* in making you the person you are? Studies of twins have come up with some clues.

In families without twins, each brother and sister inherits different qualities from their mothers and fathers. Identical twins — the twins that develop from a single egg and a single sperm — inherit exactly the same qualities from parents. But as the interviews in the last chapter show, identical twins are different from each other in many ways.

If they inherited the same qualities, why are they different? Maybe you can guess: because of their environment. They started becoming different people back when they were living in different parts of the uterus. Then, when the twins were babies, parents sometimes babbled at one and sang to the other. As the babies became toddling children, other children learned to tell them apart and treat each one slightly differently. Each became more of a different person because of the environment. But even as these differences develop, twins remain alike in some ways because of what they inherited.

So if you are a scientist who wants to know what qualities people inherit, one place to begin is to find out how identical twins are very much alike — more alike than nontwin brothers and sisters or fraternal twins. The basic idea is that when identical twins look more alike than other nontwin relatives, they have inherited their nearly identical looks. And, along the same lines of thinking, when identical twins *act* more alike compared with, say, fraternal twins, then the identical twins have inherited a tendency to act that way. When scientists find clear evidence of such tendencies in identical twins, they conclude that the tendency in general can be passed on from parents to children, whether the children are twins or not.

Here's one example to make it clearer — and the example gives some clues about the questions asked at the beginning of the chapter.

Scientists Robert Plomin and David C. Rowe of the University of Colorado wanted to learn more about why people think and behave the way they do. They turned for help to a special set of mothers — mothers of twins.

Many such mothers belong to a Mothers of Twins Club. There are more than 225 of these clubs, in 45 of the 50 states. (The national office is at 5402 Amberwood Lane, Rockville, Maryland 20853.) These organizations have more than 9,000 mem-

(37)

Fifteen pairs of twins posed for the
camera at a recent Mothers of Twins Club
meeting in Pennsylvania.

bers, and their membership is constantly growing. Clubs allow mothers of twins to exchange information about rearing twins. (For instance, mothers learn to feed infant twins from the same dish with the same spoon. Twins share all their germs anyway, and the one-dish routine saves clean-up time.) Often, clubs sponsor parties for twins and parents.

The clubs frequently perform other work for science. They supply twins for study. It was natural for Plomin and Rowe to begin their research by calling on mothers of twins for help.

Their plan was to compare sets of identical twins with sets of fraternal twins. Identicals, remember, come from the same egg. Each identical twin inherits the same qualities as the other twin. Fraternal twins, from different eggs, inherit different qualities, just like any set of nontwin brothers or sisters. But both kinds of twins in the study, fraternal and identical, grew up as pairs, each pair in the same environment. Plomin and Rowe planned to study whether identical twins were more alike than fraternal twins in the way they behaved. If the identicals were more alike than the fraternals in some ways, then the scientists could conclude that those ways were inherited from parents.

The two researchers asked the mothers of ninety-one pairs of twins — thirty-six of the pairs identicals — to rate their children. Each mother completed a written report on each child. The reports gave a simple portrait of every twin, telling, for example, how active the child tended to be, whether the child stuck to a task until it was completed, and whether the twin often disliked food. Then Plomin and Rowe studied the reports, looking for similarities and differences.

They found that identical twins were much more alike than fraternals in several ways. Identicals tended to be quite similar in the way they reacted when they were crying and a parent tried to comfort them. In many cases, if hugging didn't help one, it probably wouldn't help the other in a similar situation, either. Fraternals weren't nearly so similar. Identicals were also much more alike than fraternals in activity: if one identical tended to be on the go all the time, the other identical would be, too. In general, identicals also reacted to outsiders in similar ways, while fraternals were more likely to have different reactions. Other differences between the two kinds of twins: identicals were more alike in how emotional they were, and in how long they were able to stick with a task before losing patience.

The study doesn't show that identical twins are more active, emotional, patient, sociable, or soothable when crying than fraternal twins. It does show that identicals tend to be more like *each other* in these temperaments than fraternal twins.

There is one major exception, the study shows. Any twin tends to have the same reaction to food as the other twin. This tendency is roughly as strong whether the twin is identical or fraternal.

What can you pick up from these findings? Maybe at this point you feel like throwing the whole puzzle away and shouting "Nothing!" This kind of study *is* pretty complicated. Scientists themselves didn't even dream of doing this kind of work until about a century ago.

Plomin and Rowe discovered a lot of information in the mothers' reports. The research showed a possibility, they said, that many of the ways children behave are passed on to them from their parents. If you tend to be very active, for instance, there's a good chance that you inherited that quality from your parents.

Even before you were born, you were set to be active. The way you react to other people, the patience or impatience you feel when you work hard at something, the emotions you feel, your ability to be comforted when you're unhappy — all of these qualities may have been shaped in you by your mother and father before birth.

Your feelings about food, however, are something else. Plomin and Rowe said the study suggested that you *learn* to like certain foods and dislike others. You aren't born hating broccoli or loving ice cream. You pick up such tastes as you grow.

The study doesn't prove that every time you feel cranky, the reason is that your parents were cranky, and that you were just born cranky. Even people who inherit part of what they are from parents can grow up quite different from mothers or fathers because of the way they are treated, because of the environment in which they live.

But the study with twins does suggest that your parents contributed important pieces to your personality before you were born, even though the pieces may be shuffled around or filed down as you grow up.

That's just one study. Other scientists have completed dozens of other studies using twins to learn more about all people. During the research, scientists have also learned more about twins themselves, for example, that the vast majority of twins grow up as healthy and happy as anyone else.

In some very rare cases, however, twins are dramatically different from normal people. They are born physically attached to each other. The next chapter is a report of their problem, and what can be done about it today.

SIAMESE TWINS

Twin brothers named Chang and Eng, born in Siam in 1811, were lucky to survive. For one thing, they were born joined to each other by a thick, flexible band running between them at the chest. The attachment made birth extremely dangerous. The second danger arose years later as word of the unusual brothers spread throughout the country (which is called Thailand today). When the Siamese king, Chowpohyi, heard about them, he believed they would bring bad luck on his country. He ordered them put to death.

But the boys had luck on their side — as well as considerable skill. They were active and athletic. A British trader named Robert Hunter, who lived in Siam, paid money for their freedom, and took them out of Siam. The twins took the name Bunker as their surname. Eventually they wound up in Boston where they were introduced to P. T. Barnum, an American showman. He hired them immediately to be a sideshow attraction in his circus.

They traveled widely with the show, drawing huge crowds of curious people. Then, at age thirty-two, they married sisters in North Carolina, set up homes in two houses, and moved every three days or so between homes and wives. And Chang and Eng Bunker fathered twenty-two children.

Considering their low chances of survival as children, their lives were a remarkable success. But problems arose when they were in their sixties. Chang had a stroke, a serious illness. He also began drinking heavily. Eng didn't drink at all and was forced to watch his brother lose his senses and his temper. Sometimes Chang broke up pieces of furniture. Sometimes he set fires. To get back at him, Eng sometimes stayed awake late into the night, playing checkers.

Then one day in 1874, Chang had a second stroke and died. There was nothing wrong with Eng at the time, but after a few hours of living attached to his dead brother, Eng died, too. To this day no one knows exactly why.

Chang and Eng were the most famous of twins born joined together. Because they were born in Siam, such twins today are still often called Siamese twins, although such pairs are born in every country. For that reason, doctors today more often call them conjoined twins. Studies from Chicago and Los Angeles indicate that on average there is one set of conjoined twins every 50,000 births. Other research from Atlanta shows an average of one conjoined set every 20,000 births. In any case, you can see, such

The Siamese twins Chang and Eng
with two of their children

(44)

twins are rare. On average, one set of twins is born every seventeen minutes, while conjoined twins are born only once every two or three days.

Conjoined twins begin something like identical twins. An egg-sperm combination begins to divide, the way it does when identicals are on the way. But then, before separation, the division stops. Two connected bodies develop.

Chang and Eng weren't the first to survive this condition. Dr. H. H. Newman of the University of Chicago reports finding evidence of conjoined twins who survived in England almost 900 years ago. Eliza and Mary Biddendon, he writes, were born in England in A.D. 1100. They were attached at the hips and shoulders, and each had only one arm. Not very much is known about them, Dr. Newman reports, but the sketchy information does include one curious fact that made the sisters similar to Chang and Eng. When one of them died, her sister quickly followed, refusing to let surgeons cut away the attachment to the dead body. Among the surviving sister's last words: "As we came together, we will also go together."

Dr. Newman tells a similar story about two conjoined sisters, Rosa and Josepha Blazek, who lived in this century. Like Chang and Eng, the twins were entertainers. One day in 1922, Josepha became seriously ill while the sisters were appearing in Chicago. They went to a hospital where a doctor examined them.

The Siamese twins Josepha and Rosa Blazek
were in great demand as entertainers.

He reported later that they were joined by a thick band in the waist region. Rosa was tall and thin while Josepha was shorter and heavier, but the doctor reported that they had learned to get along well. As youngsters, they told the doctor, they had even learned to climb trees. As adults, they were skilled and intelligent. Both spoke several languages. Both played the violin.

That day in the hospital, Josepha was dangerously sick with jaundice, a disease that discolors the skin, turning it yellowish. The doctor reported that Rosa was healthy. When Josepha's condition worsened, the doctor advised risking surgery to cut them apart, because he knew that Rosa would not survive attached to a dead body. But the twin's manager, who was also their brother, refused to permit the operation. His sisters were star attractions — when they were attached. Separated, they would draw no crowds. Josepha died on March 30, 1922. Rosa died a day or so later, as doctors had known she would.

In recent years, doctors have been able to offer some conjoined twins more than mere survival, or life as a circus attraction. Surgical techniques have improved to the point where in some cases surgeons can cut even extensive attachments between the two bodies, permitting each twin to live free and separate.

Brenda and Linda McCall, for instance, born in March, 1976, were connected from chest to navel. Once, they would have been forced to go through life facing each other, permanently attached. But when the girls were six months old, they were given a chance for a normal life.

The operation Brenda and Linda had was complicated. The surgeon had to cut the attachment without damaging the life-supporting organs of either child. Before the operation, two teams of fifteen doctors, nurses, and technicians, headed by Dr. Kenneth

Kenigsberg, practiced what they would do. They rehearsed every movement in the forty-seven-step operation three times, using realistic baby dolls sewed together to make the practice sessions seem real. They estimated the operation would take four and a half hours.

During the actual operation, doctors followed detailed plans. Cutting through the attachment was only part of the problem; the doctors also had to move parts of some organs into proper positions in each child's body. The practice was worthwhile. The operation ended successfully, almost four and a half hours after it had begun.

After the operation, hospital personnel put other plans into effect to help the twins adjust. They fed both children at the same time so neither would feel alone. Sometimes they placed them face to face on the bed so the twins would feel the warmth and closeness they had experienced as newborns.

Once, twins like these might have gone through life as oddities, appearing on stage so audiences could stare. Today, the attention paid to them is healthier. Brenda and Linda are famous because they are separate and normal children — Siamese twins no more.

7 "SUPERTWINS" AND EVERYDAY TRIPLETS

At 4 A.M. on the morning of May 28, 1934, Elzire Dionne delivered a baby girl after three hours of labor in the family's farmhouse in North Bay, Canada. There was no doctor there at the time. Mrs. Labelle, a midwife — a woman trained to deliver babies — carried the newborn close to an oven to warm her, then set the baby down in a tub, and covered her with woolen bedclothes.

Almost immediately, Mrs. Dionne needed Mrs. Labelle again. Another little girl was on its way. The second child, identical to the first, was born before Dr. Allan Dafoe had arrived.

"Put on some more hot water," Dr. Dafoe said to Mrs. Labelle. A third child was being born. Then came a fourth. Within minutes, a fifth had arrived. All were identical — all five had come from one egg.

The five children born that day — Annette, Cecile, Emilie, Marie, and Yvonne — were tiny. The largest, Yvonne, weighed

(51)

less than 3 pounds (1.4 kg), and the smallest, Marie, less than 2 pounds (.9 kg). The doctor was seriously worried about their survival. Even after a week or two, Marie and Emilie occasionally turned blue, a sign that their bodies were not getting enough oxygen. Frail as they were, though, the five created a worldwide sensation greater than any of Barnum's circuses, with or without Siamese twins.

The Dionne sisters — all five survived childhood and three are alive today — are the best-known group of what are sometimes called "Supertwins," sets of more than two children born at the same time. In the United States, there were 1,086 such "multiple births" reported in 1976 (the latest year for which figures were available), an average of about three a day.

In most of these multiple births, mothers deliver triplets, sets of three children. Quadruplets — sets of four children — are much more rare, and quintuplets like the Dionnes are rarer still. At the time they were born, one scientist — Dr. Norman Ford of Toronto — found only 53 confirmed cases of quintuplets born over the previous three centuries. In only two of the 53 cases were the babies identical. (*The Guiness Book of Records* reports that since 1900, 23 cases of sextuplets — six children born at the same time — have been reported. During the same period, the book reports, there have been 19 cases of seven children born at once, five cases of eight children, and two of nonuplets — nine children at one birth.)

Multiple births result from any one of many different conditions. In some cases, the mother produces three or more eggs in one month, and each combines with a different sperm from the father. The result is three or more nonidentical children. Sometimes a mother releases two eggs; both combine with sperm, and then one divides. The result: triplets, including two identical twins and one nonidentical child. Sometimes one egg divides into three or more sections, resulting in a crowd of identical babies.

What's it like to be a "Supertwin"? From newspaper and film stories about the Dionnes published during the 1930s and 1940s, you would have guessed it was like having a birthday every day. Later on, the sisters themselves told what it was really like.

The stories presented five carefree little girls. For years after they were born, their faces appeared in movies and magazines, with stories and advertisements. Dolls were modeled after them. Their pictures appeared on aluminum toy tea sets. At one time or another, their names were used to sell toothpaste, breakfast cereal, milk, soap, and germ killer. By the time they were two, they had made a quarter of a million dollars. A few years after that, in 1940 when they were six, their fortune had risen to almost a million dollars.

"As years pass and the little girls become trained in the arts of public entertainment," wrote Dr. Newman when the girls were eight, "they will probably be even a greater attraction than they are now." He continued with his predictions: "That they will always be in the public eye seems to be inevitable. What else can they do? The only alternative would be to hide them in a convent, and for many reasons that is not at all likely to happen."

What did happen, however, ran totally against Newman's predictions. Public interest in the quintuplets began to decline as the United States entered World War II. Products stamped with their faces no longer sold. The flow of income slowed. Reports from the twins themselves later revealed that during the years when their lives appeared to be a continuous party, they were suffering.

Dr. Dafoe had removed them early in life from their parents'

On their first birthday each
of the Dionne quintuplets
celebrated with a cake of her own.
Photographers followed the
Dionne quintuplets around when
they visited New York City
in 1950 — snapping pictures of
them even on the subway.

farmhouse and put them into a private hospital where they were raised by nurses. Here, they were regularly put on display for thousands of visitors who came to stare as they played in a specially designed playground. When they misbehaved, they were put in another specially designed room, by themselves.

When they were nine years old, the quintuplets finally got back together with their parents, but the reunion wasn't happy, the sisters said later. Their parents seemed to resent them. Their home was sad. Eventually, Marie, Emilie, and Yvonne did just what Dr. Newman said they would never do: they decided they wanted to become nuns. (Yvonne was the only one who actually did.) By then, the public had lost interest in them. Emilie died in 1954 and Marie in 1970, and their deaths roused little attention.

Pierre Berton, a Canadian journalist, reports that today the three survivors are seldom recognized in the Montreal suburb where they live. Yvonne does volunteer work in a public library. Annette, divorced from her husband, has four children. Cecile works in a local supermarket, Berton reports.

The Dionne sisters were caught in a carnival of public attention that isn't likely to be repeated. For one thing, beginning in the mid-1960s, doctors began using a new treatment for women who had difficulty having children. The doctors prescribed hormones — substances that sometimes stimulated the release of several eggs at a time. The number of multiple births rose. In 1965 alone, two sets of quintuplets, three sets of quadruplets, and many triplets and twins were born as a result of the new treatment. "Supertwins," in other words, became much more common.

At the same time, the Dionnes' own report — in a book called *We Were Five* — and later reports like Berton's have helped make people more aware of the danger and cruelty of treating people

Sometimes these triplets dress alike
and enjoy the confusion that creates.

born at the same time as sideshow attractions. Just as twins I talked with (at around age eleven or twelve) stressed that they wanted to be recognized as separate people, many triplets resent taking parts in a trio all the time.

"Everyone on this block thinks we're one person, cloned," Karen Wozniak of New York told me in an interview. Karen and her sisters Susanne and Valerie are triplets, born October 17, 1966. In school, Karen said, other students sometimes holler, "Hey, triplets!" at them.

"We yell back, 'Hey, singles!'" she said.

Sometimes, Susanne said, people they pass on the street stop the three sisters and ask, "Are you *twins*?" And once in a Burger King restaurant, someone asked for their autographs.

Karen, Susanne, and Valerie are alike in some ways. They all like pizza and vanilla ice cream. Sometimes their minds seem to work alike.

"One time I was thinking of a tune and Susanne started to sing it," Valerie said. Susanne said sometimes they tell stories as a team. "One of us starts a story, one comes in with the middle part and the third one comes in with the ending," Susanne said.

But each of the sisters is growing up to be a different person, setting off on her own from the team. "It used to be that you couldn't invite one without inviting all three," Mrs. Wozniak said. "At one time in their lives, if somebody invited one out, the other two would be very hurt and upset. Now that they're older, they're changing. They're individuals with their own friends."

Suzanne: "We *look* totally different."

Karen: "I like staying apart from Susanne and Valerie as much as possible. I work things out by myself."

Valerie: "I wish people would stop calling us twins and triplets."

Of course many other triplets and twins go through their entire lives as a close team. Some twins and triplets continue to dress in the same kinds of clothes long after their parents stop choosing what they wear. The point is, triplets today don't have to put on "Supertwin" costumes the way the Dionnes did. Twins don't have to be odd, or cute, to make friends. They don't have to perform or play roles or act out other people's stories. Their own true stories, unpredictable as they grow and learn, are much more interesting.

FOR FURTHER INFORMATION

Material in this book comes from articles, books, and personal interviews. In this list of references, entries marked with an asterisk (*) tend to be easy to find and fun to read. Your librarian can probably help you locate them quickly — or other information on twins — even if these titles don't show up in your library's card catalog.

ARTICLES

Beit-Hallahmi, Benjamin and Paluszy, Maria. Twinship in Mythology and Science: Ambivalence, Differentiation, and the Magical Bond. *Comprehensive Psychiatry*, July/August, 1974, 345–353.

*Berton, Pierre. The Dionne Years. *The New York Times Magazine*, April 23, 1978, 12–15.

Hanson, James W. Incidence of Conjoined Twinning. *The Lancet*, December 20, 1975, 1257.

*Kent, George. The Case of the Third Twin. *Reader's Digest*, November, 1951, 18–23.

Paluszny, Maria. Queries that Mothers of Twins Put to Their Doctors. *Clinical Pediatrics*, July, 1975, 624–626.

Plomin, Robert and Rowe, David C. A Twin Study of Temperament in Young Children. *The Journal of Psychology*, 97, 1977, 107–113.

*Successful Separation; Six-Months Old Siamese Twins Are Now Expected to Live Normal, Healthy, Happy Lives. *Ebony*, December, 1977, 123–124.

Stevenson, Isobel. Twins Among Primitive Peoples. *Ciba Symposia*, January, 1941, 702–705.

BOOKS

Bulmer, M. G. *The Biology of Twinning in Man*. Oxford: Clarendon Press, 1970.

*Hagedorn, Judy W. and Kizziar, Janet. *Gemini; The Psychology and Phenomena of Twins*. Anderson, S. C.: Droke House/Hallux, 1974.

*Lindeman, Bard. *The Twins Who Found Each Other*. New York: Morrow, 1969.

Gedda, Luigi. *Twins in History and Science*. Springfield, Ill.: Charles C Thomas, 1961.

Newman, Horatio Hackett. *Twins and Super-Twins*. New York: Hutchinson's Scientific and Technical Publications, 1942.

Papalia, Diane and Olds, Dally Wendkos. *A Child's World*. New York: McGraw-Hill, 1975.

*Scheinfeld, Amram. *Twins and Supertwins*. Philadelphia: J. B. Lippincott Co., 1967.

ORGANIZATIONS

International Twins Association. This group calls its 300 members together once a year in an American city so twins can meet each other, go to theaters or athletic events, or take tours. The association was formed in the 1930s. Membership costs $2.50 for twins under twelve, $5 for members twelve to twenty-one, and $10 for adults. C/o Dr. Judy Hagedorn, 3000 East Skelly Drive, Suite 315, Tulsa, Oklahoma 74105.

The National Organization of Mothers of Twins Clubs. There are 228 Mothers of Twins Clubs. The idea for the clubs — to allow mothers of twins to share experiences and offer help and encouragement to each other — began in Canton, Ohio, in 1960 and has now spread to 45 of the 50 states. The clubs have some 9,000 members. 5402 Amberwood Lane, Rockville, Maryland 20853.

INDEX